Samsung Galaxy S23

SENIORS GUIDE

2023

The Most Complete and Updated Manual for the Non-Tech-Savvy to Master your Brand New Smartphone in No Time

John Halbert

Table of Contents

Introduction

Welcome to "Samsung Galaxy S23 for Seniors: The Most Complete and Updated Manual to Master your Brand New Smartphone in No Time as a Non-Tech Savvy"! This book is specifically designed for seniors and non-tech-savvy individuals who are looking to make the most of their new Samsung Galaxy S23 smartphone. We understand that technology can sometimes be overwhelming, especially when you're trying to learn the ins and outs of a new device. That's why we've created this comprehensive guide to help you navigate your way through the exciting features and functionalities of the Samsung Galaxy S23 with ease.

The Samsung Galaxy S23 is an incredible smartphone packed with cutting-edge features and powerful performance capabilities that make it a top choice for users of all ages. However, for seniors who may not be as familiar with technology, the sheer number of options and settings can be daunting. With this book, our aim is to break down the complexities of the Samsung Galaxy S23 and make it easily accessible for everyone, regardless of your technical expertise.

Throughout this book, we'll be covering a wide range of topics, starting with an introduction to the Samsung Galaxy S23, its interface, and how to customize settings to meet your individual needs. You'll learn about using the camera, understanding battery life and charging, as well as troubleshooting common issues you may encounter. We'll also discuss how to stay safe and secure online and explore the various communication and connectivity features available on the Samsung Galaxy S23.

As you progress through the chapters, you'll discover the advanced features and functions that the Samsung Galaxy S23 has to offer, including customizing your device with apps and widgets, managing and organizing files and media, and using accessibility features designed specifically for seniors. We'll even guide you through setting up Samsung Pay and other mobile payment methods and show you how to manage your health and wellness using the device's built-in features.

In the entertainment and leisure section, we'll explore various ways you can enjoy your Samsung Galaxy S23, from streaming movies and music to playing games and reading e-books. To ensure that you're always up-to-date, we'll also cover the latest updates and upgrades for your device. And as a bonus, we'll provide you with a special chapter on using Android Auto in your car, so you can get the most out of your smartphone even when you're on the go.

We've designed this book to be as user-friendly and engaging as possible, with clear step-by-step instructions, helpful tips, and easy-to-follow explanations. Regardless of your experience with smartphones or technology in general, we're confident that this book will serve as your go-to guide for mastering the Samsung Galaxy S23.

So, let's get started on this exciting journey of discovery! As you read through the chapters and begin to explore the many features and functionalities of the Samsung Galaxy S23, you'll quickly see that this powerful device has the potential to enhance your daily life in countless ways. Whether you're looking to stay connected with loved ones, manage your personal and professional schedules, or simply enjoy a world of entertainment at your fingertips, the Samsung Galaxy S23 is the perfect companion to help you achieve your goals.

With this book as your guide, you'll be well on your way to unlocking the full potential of your Samsung Galaxy S23 and embracing the world of technology with confidence. So, sit back, relax, and prepare to embark on an incredible journey that will empower you to make the most of your Samsung Galaxy S23 smartphone, no matter your level of tech-savviness. Happy exploring!

Chapter 1: Getting Started

Introduction to the Samsung Galaxy S23

Welcome to Chapter 2! In this chapter, we will begin our journey with the Samsung Galaxy S23 by introducing you to its key features and specifications. The Samsung Galaxy S23 is a state-of-the-art smartphone designed to offer a seamless and enjoyable user experience. Equipped with a powerful processor, ample storage, and an impressive camera system, the Galaxy S23 is a top-of-the-line device that caters to users of all ages and experience levels.

Key Features and Specifications

- Display: The Samsung Galaxy S23 boasts a stunning 6.1-inch Dynamic AMOLED display with a resolution of 3200 x 1440 pixels. This high-resolution screen ensures that images, videos, and text appear crisp and clear, providing an immersive viewing experience.

- Processor: Powered by an advanced Exynos or Snapdragon processor (depending on your region), the Galaxy S23 is designed for lightning-fast performance and smooth multitasking.

- Memory and Storage: The device comes in various configurations, offering up to 12GB of RAM and up to 512GB of internal storage. This ample storage space allows you to store plenty of apps, photos, videos, and documents without worrying about running out of space.

- Camera: The Samsung Galaxy S23 features an advanced camera system comprising a 108-megapixel primary lens, a 12-megapixel ultra-wide lens, and a 10-megapixel telephoto lens. This versatile camera setup allows you to capture stunning photos and videos in a variety of scenarios.

- Battery: Equipped with a large 5,000mAh battery, the Galaxy S23 is designed to last all day on a single charge, even with heavy usage.

- Connectivity: The Samsung Galaxy S23 supports 5G connectivity, ensuring fast internet speeds and seamless online experiences.

Samsung Galaxy S23 Variants

Display:

- Galaxy S23: 6.1" FHD+ Dynamic AMOLED 2x, 120Hz Adaptive Refresh Rate, 425ppi, 1,750nit (outdoor peak)

- Galaxy S23+: 6.6" FHD+ Dynamic AMOLED 2x, 120Hz Adaptive Refresh Rate, 393ppi, 1,750nit (outdoor peak)

- Galaxy S23 Ultra: 6.8" QHD+ Dynamic AMOLED 2x, 120Hz Adaptive Refresh Rate, 500ppi, 1,750nit (outdoor peak)

The Ultra model has the largest display, making it ideal for users who prioritize screen real estate for tasks like watching videos or playing games. The S23 and S23 Plus offer slightly smaller displays, catering to users who prefer a more compact form factor.

Camera:

- Galaxy S23 & S23+: 50MP f/1.8 primary, Dual Pixel AF, OIS; 12MP f/2.2 ultra-wide (120° FoV); 10MP f/2.4 3x optical zoom sensor with OIS; 30x space zoom

- Galaxy S23 Ultra: 200MP f/1.7 primary, OIS and PDAF; 12MP f/2.2 ultra-wide (120° FoV); 10MP f/2.4 3x optical zoom sensor with OIS; 10MP f/4.9 10x optical zoom with OIS; 100x space zoom

The S23 Ultra's camera system has more advanced capabilities than the other models, offering improved zoom and overall performance. The S23 and S23 Plus feature a high-quality triple camera system that will still cater to most users' photography needs.

Battery Capacity:

- Galaxy S23: 3,900mAh, 25W fast charging, 15W wireless charging, Reverse wireless charging
- Galaxy S23+: 4,700mAh, 45W fast charging, 15W wireless charging, Reverse wireless charging
- Galaxy S23 Ultra: 5,000mAh, 45W fast charging, 15W wireless charging, Reverse wireless charging

Battery capacity increases with each model, with the S23 Ultra offering the largest battery for extended usage between charges. The S23 and S23 Plus have smaller batteries, but they should still provide adequate battery life for most users.

S Pen Compatibility:

- Samsung Galaxy S23 and S23 Plus: No S Pen support
- Samsung Galaxy S23 Ultra: S Pen support

Only the S23 Ultra supports the use of an S Pen, making it an attractive option for users who enjoy taking notes, drawing, or using the stylus for increased precision.

Price

- Galaxy S23: Starting at $799.99
- Galaxy S23+: Starting at $999.99
- Galaxy S23 Ultra: Starting at $1,199.99

The Samsung Galaxy S23 Ultra will likely have the highest price tag due to its premium features and capabilities, followed by the S23 Plus and then the base S23 model. Users should consider their budget and specific needs when choosing between these three devices.

Device Weight and Dimensions

- Galaxy S23: 70.9 x 146.3 x 7.6mm, 168g, IP68 certified
- Galaxy S23+: 76.2 x 157.7 x 7.6mm, 196g, IP68 certified

- Galaxy S23 Ultra: 77.9 x 163.3 x 8.9 mm, 233g, IP68 certified

These dimensions and weights provide an overview of the size differences among the Samsung Galaxy S23, S23 Plus, and S23 Ultra models.

Each model will have slightly different dimensions and weights due to their varying display sizes and internal components. Larger models like the S23 Ultra may be more difficult for some seniors to handle comfortably due to their size and weight. On the other hand, smaller models like the S23 may be more manageable for everyday use.

Memory and Storage Options

- Galaxy S23: 8+128GB, 8+256GB (UFS 3.1)
- Galaxy S23+: 8+256GB, 8+512GB (UFS 4.0)
- Galaxy S23 Ultra: 8+256GB, 12+512GB, 12GB+1TB (UFS 4.0)

The different models may also offer varying memory and storage options. For example, the base model S23 could come with lower internal storage capacities compared to the S23 Plus or S23 Ultra. This might impact the number of apps, photos, and other files that users can store on their devices. Seniors should consider their storage needs when selecting a model.

Performance

Although all models in the S23 lineup will offer excellent performance, the S23 Ultra might feature a slightly more powerful processor or additional RAM, resulting in faster and smoother device operation. This could be particularly beneficial for users who require more processing power for multitasking or running demanding apps.

Color Options and Material Finishes

The Samsung Galaxy S23, S23 Plus, and S23 Ultra may be available in different color options and material finishes. While this may not impact the functionality of the device, personal preferences, and aesthetic considerations may play a role in the decision-making process for seniors.

Software Features

While the core software experience should be similar across all S23 models, there might be some exclusive features or settings available only on the higher-end models like the S23 Ultra. Seniors should review these additional features to determine if they are essential for their needs.

These differences represent some of the main distinctions between the Samsung Galaxy S23, S23 Plus, and S23 Ultra. Users should carefully consider their priorities and preferences, such as display size, camera capabilities, battery life, and additional features like S Pen support when deciding which model best suits their needs.

In the book "Samsung Galaxy S23 for Seniors," the main focus is to help seniors and non-tech-savvy users master their new smartphones, regardless of the specific model they choose. The differences outlined above, along with the previously discussed variations, should provide a comprehensive understanding of the distinctions between the Samsung Galaxy S23, S23 Plus, and S23 Ultra models.

Setting up your Device

Setting up your Samsung Galaxy S23 is a straightforward process that ensures your device is configured correctly and ready to use. In this section, we will walk you through the initial setup process, including inserting the SIM card, powering the device, and configuring essential settings.

1. Inserting the SIM Card

Before turning on your Samsung Galaxy S23, you will need to insert your SIM card to connect to your mobile network and access phone and data services. The device uses a nano-SIM card, and you will find a SIM card ejector tool included in the box to help you insert the card.

- Locate the SIM card tray on the top edge of the device.
- Using the ejector tool, gently push the pin into the hole next to the tray to release it.
- Remove the tray and place your nano-SIM card into the appropriate slot, ensuring the gold contacts are facing down.
- Carefully reinsert the tray back into the device, making sure it's aligned correctly.

2. Powering on the Device

To turn on your Samsung Galaxy S23, press and hold the Power button located on the right side of the device until the Samsung logo appears on the screen. Once the device powers on, you will be guided through the initial setup process.

3. Selecting Language and Region

The first step of the setup process is selecting your preferred language and region. This will ensure that your device's interface, keyboard, and other features are configured for your location and language preferences.

4. Connecting to Wi-Fi

During the setup process, you will be prompted to connect to a Wi-Fi network. This is essential for downloading updates, setting up your Google account, and accessing various features and services. Select your Wi-Fi network from the list, enter the password, and tap "Connect."

5. Setting up Google Account

To access the full range of features and services offered by your Samsung Galaxy S23, you will need to sign in to your Google account or create a new one. This account allows you to sync your contacts, email, calendar, and other data across your devices and use various Google services, such as the Google Play Store, Google Maps, and Google Assistant.

6. Protecting Your Device

During the setup process, you will be prompted to set up a screen lock to protect your device from unauthorized access. You can choose from several security options, including PIN, password, pattern, fingerprint, or facial recognition. We recommend setting up a strong, unique password or PIN and enabling fingerprint or facial recognition for added security.

7. Restoring and Transferring Data

If you have data from a previous device that you would like to transfer to your Samsung Galaxy S23, you can use the Smart Switch app during the setup process. This app allows you to transfer data, such as contacts, messages, photos, and apps, from your old device to your new one, ensuring a seamless transition.

8. Customizing Device Settings

Once you have completed the initial setup process, you can further customize your Samsung Galaxy S23 by adjusting various settings to meet your needs and preferences. This may include setting up notifications, configuring display and sound settings, and personalizing the Home screen with your favorite apps and widgets.

By following these steps, you can successfully set up your Samsung Galaxy S23 and ensure that it is properly configured for your individual needs.

Navigating the Device's Interface

The Samsung Galaxy S23 runs on the Android operating system, which features a user-friendly interface designed for easy navigation. In this section, we will guide you through the basic elements of the Galaxy S23's interface, helping you become familiar with its layout and functionality.

- Home Screen: The Home Screen is the main screen of your Samsung Galaxy S23, displaying your most-used apps and widgets. You can customize the Home Screen by adding, removing, or rearranging apps and widgets to suit your preferences.

- Notification Panel: To access the Notification Panel, swipe down from the top of the screen. The Notification Panel displays your latest notifications and provides quick access to commonly used settings, such as Wi-Fi, Bluetooth, and Airplane Mode.

- App Drawer: The App Drawer contains all the apps installed on your device. To access the App Drawer, swipe up from the bottom of the Home Screen. You can search for apps, create folders, and arrange apps alphabetically or in a custom order within the App Drawer.

- Navigation Buttons: At the screen bottom, you'll find three navigation buttons – Back, Home, and Recent Apps. The Back button takes you to the previous screen, the Home button returns you to the Home Screen, whereas the Recent Apps button displays a list of your recently used apps.

Customizing Settings to Meet Individual Needs

The Samsung Galaxy S23 offers a wide range of settings that can be customized to suit your individual needs and preferences. In this section, we will explore some of the key settings that you can adjust to personalize your device.

- Display Settings: To access the Display settings, go to Settings > Display. Here, you can adjust various display-related settings, such as brightness, screen timeout, and font size. You can also enable Dark mode, which changes the background color to a darker shade, making it easier on your eyes and conserving battery life.

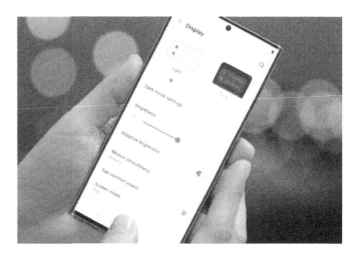

- Sound and Vibration Settings: To customize your device's audio settings, navigate to Settings > Sound and Vibration. In this menu, you can adjust the volume levels for ringtones, notifications, and media. You can also set custom ringtones, enable or disable vibration, and customize system sounds.

- Notification Settings: To manage your notifications, go to Settings > Notifications. Here, you can choose which apps are allowed to send notifications, customize notification styles, and enable or disable specific notification features, such as notification badges or the notification LED.

- Security Settings: To enhance the security of your device, navigate to Settings > Biometrics and Security. You can set up various security features, such as face recognition, fingerprint scanning, or a PIN, password, or pattern lock. You can also manage privacy settings, control app permissions, and enable features like Find My Mobile, which allows you to locate, lock, or erase your device remotely if it's lost or stolen.

- Accessibility Settings: To make your Samsung Galaxy S23 more accessible, go to Settings > Accessibility. This menu contains various features designed to assist users with disabilities or specific needs. Some of the available options include font size and style adjustments, screen magnification, color correction, and hearing aid compatibility.

- Customizing the Home Screen: To personalize your Home Screen, tap and hold on an empty space, and you will see options to change wallpapers, themes, and home screen settings. You can add or remove app icons, create folders, and customize widgets to create a Home Screen layout that best suits your needs.

By exploring and customizing these settings, you can tailor your Samsung Galaxy S23 to meet your individual needs and preferences, creating a more enjoyable and efficient user experience.

In conclusion, getting started with your Samsung Galaxy S23 involves familiarizing yourself with the device's interface, key features, and various settings that can be customized to suit your needs. As you become more comfortable navigating your new smartphone, you'll be able to unlock its full potential and enjoy all the incredible features it has to offer. In the following chapters, we will dive deeper into specific features and functionalities, helping you make the most of your Samsung Galaxy S23 experience.

Chapter 2: Camera and Hardware

In this chapter, we will delve into the camera and hardware features of the Samsung Galaxy S23. We will discuss how to use the camera effectively and explore other hardware features of the device, such as battery life and charging. By the end of this chapter, you will have a comprehensive understanding of the Galaxy S23's camera and hardware capabilities.

Using the Camera and Other Hardware Features

The Samsung Galaxy S23 boasts an impressive camera system designed to capture stunning images and videos in various lighting conditions and scenarios. In this section, we will explore the different camera features and provide tips on how to get the most out of your Galaxy S23's camera.

Camera Overview

The Samsung Galaxy S23 comes equipped with an impressive camera system designed to capture stunning photos and videos. Its high-quality camera hardware, and advanced software features enable users to capture professional-level images and record high-resolution videos with ease. Here's an overview of the camera specifications for the Samsung Galaxy S23:

Rear Cameras

- Primary Camera: A 50MP f/1.8 lens with Dual Pixel autofocus and optical image stabilization (OIS) for crisp and clear images.
- Ultra-Wide Camera: A 12MP f/2.2 lens with a 120° field of view, perfect for capturing landscapes and group photos.
- Telephoto Camera: A 10MP f/2.4 lens with 3x optical zoom and OIS, allowing you to capture distant subjects with great detail.

In addition to these lenses, the Galaxy S23 also offers up to 30x space zoom for even more extended reach.

Front Camera

- A 12MP f/2.2 lens with phase-detection autofocus (PDAF) for capturing sharp selfies and enabling clear video calls.

Accessing the Camera

To access the camera on your Samsung Galaxy S23, you can either tap the Camera app icon on your Home Screen or App Drawer or use the Quick Launch feature by quickly pressing the Power button twice.

Camera Modes and Settings

The Samsung Galaxy S23 offers a wide range of camera modes and settings that cater to various shooting scenarios, enabling you to capture the perfect shot in any situation. In this section, we will discuss the different camera modes and settings available on the Galaxy S23, providing you with the tools to make the most of your device's camera capabilities.

- Photo: The default mode for capturing still images is Photo mode. In this mode, the Galaxy S23 automatically adjusts settings such as focus, exposure, and white balance to produce high-quality images. You can also tap on the subject in the viewfinder to focus on them and adjust the exposure accordingly.
- Video Mode: The Video mode allows you to record high-quality videos at various resolutions and frame rates, including 8K, 4K, and Full HD. To access Video mode, swipe

left or right on the viewfinder until you reach the desired mode. You can adjust the video resolution and frame rate in the camera settings by tapping the gear icon in the top corner of the camera app.

- Pro Mode: Pro mode provides manual controls for advanced users, allowing you to adjust settings such as ISO, shutter speed, focus, and white balance. This mode is perfect for photographers looking for more control over their images. To access Pro mode, swipe left or right on the viewfinder and select "Pro."

- Portrait Mode: Portrait mode captures photos with a blurred background, creating a professional-looking depth-of-field effect. This mode is perfect for taking portraits of people, pets, or other subjects where you want to emphasize the subject and separate them from the background. To access Portrait mode, swipe left or right on the viewfinder and select "Portrait."

- Night Mode: Night mode optimizes the camera settings for low-light conditions, producing brighter and clearer images. The Galaxy S23 uses AI technology and long exposure techniques to capture more light and reduce noise in your photos. To access Night mode, swipe left or right on the viewfinder and select "Night."

- Panorama Mode: Panorama mode allows you to capture wide-angle shots by stitching multiple images together. This mode is perfect for photographing landscapes, cityscapes, or other expansive scenes. To access Panorama mode, swipe left or right on the viewfinder and select "Panorama."

- Slow Motion Mode: Slow Motion mode records videos in slow motion, highlighting fast-moving subjects or actions. This mode is perfect for capturing sports, action scenes, or any situation where you want to emphasize movement. To access Slow Motion mode, swipe left or right on the viewfinder and select "Slow Motion."

To switch between camera modes, simply swipe left or right on the viewfinder. To access additional camera settings, tap the gear icon in the top corner of the camera app. Here, you can adjust settings like resolution, aspect ratio, timer, and more. By familiarizing yourself with the various camera modes and settings on the Samsung Galaxy S23, you can enhance your photography skills and capture stunning images and videos in any situation.

Camera Tips and Tricks

Here are some tips and tricks to help you capture stunning images and videos with your Samsung Galaxy S23:

- Use gridlines: Enable gridlines in the camera settings to help you compose your shots using the rule of thirds, a photography principle that can enhance the visual appeal of your images.

- Tap to focus: Tap on your subject in the viewfinder to focus on them and adjust the exposure accordingly. You can also lock the focus and exposure by tapping and holding on the subject.

- Use HDR: High Dynamic Range (HDR) mode captures multiple exposures and combines them into a single image, resulting in more balanced lighting and richer colors.

- Experiment with filters and effects: The Galaxy S23 offers various filters and effects that you can apply to your images and videos in real time. Tap the filter icon in the camera app to explore these options.

- Utilize the ultra-wide and telephoto lenses: Switch between the primary, ultra-wide, and telephoto lenses by tapping the corresponding icons in the camera app. This allows you to capture different perspectives and focal lengths without moving your position.

- Use Pro Mode: Pro mode on Samsung Galaxy S23 allows you to manually adjust settings like shutter speed, ISO, and white balance to capture professional-quality photos. To activate Pro mode, open the camera app, swipe to the right until you see "Pro" mode, and tap on it.

- Use Night mode: Night mode is a great feature for capturing low-light photos. It works by taking multiple photos at different exposures and combining them into a single well-lit image. To use Night mode, simply switch to the camera's Night mode and hold the camera steady for a few seconds while it captures the image.

- Use Portrait mode: Portrait mode is a great feature for taking photos of people or pets. It blurs the background to make the subject stand out. To use Portrait mode, simply switch to Portrait mode, frame your subject, and take the photo.

- Use Super Slow-mo: Samsung Galaxy S23 allows you to capture slow-motion videos at up to 960 frames per second. To use Super Slow-mo, switch to the camera's Super Slow-mo mode, select the area of the screen you want to capture and press the record button.

- Use Single Take: Single Take is a feature that captures multiple photos and videos in one go. It works by taking a 15-second video and then automatically generating multiple photos and videos from it. To use Single Take, switch to the camera's Single Take mode and press the record button.

- Use Zoom: Samsung Galaxy S23's camera has both optical and digital zoom. Optical zoom works by physically moving the lens closer to the subject, while digital zoom enlarges the image digitally. To use optical zoom, simply pinch to zoom in or out. To use digital zoom, swipe up or down on the screen.

- Use Selfie mode: Samsung Galaxy S23's front-facing camera is great for taking selfies. To use Selfie mode, switch to the front-facing camera and frame your shot. You can also use features like Portrait mode and Night mode to capture better selfies

- Use AR Emoji: AR Emoji is a feature that lets you create an animated version of yourself or someone else. To use AR Emoji, switch to the camera's AR Emoji mode, select the character you want to create and follow the on-screen instructions.

These are some of the camera tips and tricks for Samsung Galaxy S23 and its variants. By using these features, you can capture stunning photos and videos that you'll be proud to share with your friends and family. For more camera tips and tricks, you can visit the link provided in the prompt.

Understanding Battery Life and Charging

The Samsung Galaxy S23 is equipped with a large 5,000mAh battery, designed to provide all-day usage on a single charge. In this section, we will discuss how to optimize your battery life and explore the device's charging capabilities.

Monitoring Battery Usage

To keep track of your Samsung Galaxy S23's battery usage, go to Settings > Battery and device care > Battery. This section displays the current battery percentage and provides an estimate of how much time is remaining before your device needs to be recharged. You can also view a breakdown of which apps and features are consuming the most battery power, helping you identify areas where you can reduce usage to extend battery life.

Optimizing Battery Life

There are several strategies you can employ to optimize your Galaxy S23's battery life:

- Lower screen brightness: Reducing your screen brightness can significantly impact battery life. Adjust the brightness by swiping down on the Notification Panel and using the brightness slider.

- Enable Dark mode: Dark mode changes the background color of your device's interface to a darker shade, reducing battery consumption on OLED displays. Enable Dark mode in Settings > Display > Dark mode.

- Use power-saving mode: The Galaxy S23 offers power-saving modes that limit certain features and functions to conserve battery life. You can enable these modes in Settings > Battery and device care > Battery > Power saving mode.

- Disable unused features: Turning off unused features, such as Bluetooth, Wi-Fi, GPS, and NFC, can help save battery life. Disable these features when not in use by swiping down on the Notification Panel and toggling the corresponding icons.

- Limit background app activity: Some apps may consume battery life by running in the background. To limit background activity, navigate to Settings > Apps, select the app in question, and tap "Battery" to adjust its background usage settings.

Charging Your Device

The Samsung Galaxy S23 supports fast charging, allowing you to quickly replenish your battery when it's running low. To charge your device, connect the USB-C cable to the charging port at the bottom of the phone and plug the other end into a wall charger or a compatible power source. The device supports up to 45W fast charging with a compatible charger, which can significantly reduce charging time compared to standard charging.

Additionally, the Galaxy S23 supports wireless charging, allowing you to charge your device by placing it on a compatible wireless charging pad. To use wireless charging, place your phone on the charging pad with the screen facing up and ensure that it is properly aligned with the charging coil. The device also features reverse wireless charging, enabling you to charge other Qi-compatible devices, such as earbuds or smartwatches, by placing them on the back of your Galaxy S23.

Wireless Charging

Wireless charging has become a popular feature on smartphones, and many users prefer it over traditional charging methods. If you are interested in wireless charging, you may be wondering if the Samsung Galaxy S23 and its variants support this feature. Here's what you need to know:

- The Samsung Galaxy S23, S23 Plus, and S23 Ultra all support wireless charging. This means that you can charge your device by simply placing it on a compatible wireless charging pad without having to plug in any cables.

- Samsung has been offering wireless charging on its flagship devices for several years, and the Galaxy S23 series continues this trend. The devices are compatible with both Qi and PMA wireless charging standards, so you can use a wide range of wireless charging pads that support these standards.

- In addition to supporting wireless charging, the Samsung Galaxy S23 series also features fast wireless charging. This means that the devices can charge at a faster rate than regular wireless charging, which is useful when you need to top up your battery quickly.

- To use wireless charging on your Samsung Galaxy S23 or its variants, you will need a compatible wireless charging pad. You can purchase these pads from a variety of retailers, including Samsung's own online store. Once you have a compatible charging pad, simply place your device on the pad to start charging wirelessly.

In summary, the Samsung Galaxy S23, S23 Plus, and S23 Ultra all support wireless charging. This feature allows you to charge your device without plugging in any cables, making it a convenient option for many users. The devices also support fast wireless charging, which enables them to charge at a faster rate than regular wireless charging.

Reverse Wireless Charging

Reverse wireless charging is a feature that allows a smartphone to act as a wireless charger for other devices. The Samsung Galaxy S23 and its variants also come with this feature, called PowerShare. Here's what you need to know about using PowerShare on your Samsung Galaxy S23:

PowerShare is a feature that lets you use your Samsung Galaxy S23 to charge other devices that support wireless charging. This includes other smartphones, smartwatches, and wireless earbuds. To use PowerShare, you need to enable the feature and place the device you want to charge on the back of your Galaxy S23.

To enable PowerShare on your Samsung Galaxy S23, follow these steps:

1. Swipe down from the top of the screen to open the Quick Settings panel.
2. Look for the "Wireless PowerShare" icon and tap on it to turn on the feature.
3. Place the device you want to charge on the back of your Samsung Galaxy S23.

The Samsung Galaxy S23 series supports PowerShare despite having a glass back. This means you can use your device to charge other devices wirelessly, even if you don't have access to a charging cable.

One thing to keep in mind is that using PowerShare will drain your Samsung Galaxy S23's battery, so it's best to use the feature only when you need to. The amount of power transferred to the other device will also depend on its battery capacity and the level of charge it already has.

Battery Replacement and Maintenance

The Samsung Galaxy S23 has a non-removable battery, which means that it cannot be easily replaced by the user. However, over time, the battery's capacity may degrade, resulting in reduced battery life. If you notice a significant decline in your device's battery performance, you can contact an authorized Samsung service center to inquire about a battery replacement.

To maintain the health and longevity of your Galaxy S23's battery, follow these guidelines:

- Avoid extreme temperatures: Exposing your device to very high or low temperatures can negatively impact battery performance and lifespan. Store and use your device in a temperature range of 32°F to 95°F (0°C to 35°C) for optimal battery health.

- Use official chargers and cables: Using third-party chargers or cables that are not certified by Samsung may damage your device or reduce charging efficiency. Always use the charger and cable that came with your device or purchase official Samsung accessories.

- Perform regular software updates: Samsung frequently releases software updates that can improve battery optimization and overall device performance. Ensure your device is up-to-date by going to Settings > Software update.

In conclusion, the Samsung Galaxy S23 offers an impressive camera system and powerful hardware features, allowing you to capture stunning images and enjoy long-lasting battery life. By understanding and utilizing these features, you can make the most of your Galaxy S23 experience.

Chapter 3: Troubleshooting and Security

In this chapter, we will explore troubleshooting common issues with the Samsung Galaxy S23 and discuss how to stay safe and secure online. By the end of this chapter, you will be better equipped to handle any problems that may arise with your device and protect your online privacy and security.

Troubleshooting Common Issues

Smartphones like the Samsung Galaxy S23 are complex devices, and issues can sometimes arise. In this section, we will cover some of the most common problems and their solutions, helping you to resolve any issues you may encounter with your Galaxy S23.

The device Won't Turn On

If your Galaxy S23 doesn't turn on, try the following steps:

1. Check the battery: Connect your device to a charger and wait a few minutes to see if it shows any signs of charging. If it does, let it charge for a while before attempting to turn it on.

2. Perform a soft reset: Press and hold the Power button and Volume Down button simultaneously for about 10 seconds. This will force the device to restart without deleting any data.

3. If neither of the above solutions works, contact Samsung Support or visit a Samsung Service Center for assistance.

Device Freezes or Becomes Unresponsive

If your device freezes or becomes unresponsive, try the following:

1. Soft reset: Press and hold the Power button and Volume Down button simultaneously for about 10 seconds to force a restart.

2. Identify problematic apps: If your device consistently freezes or becomes unresponsive while using a specific app, try uninstalling and reinstalling the app. If the issue persists, consider finding an alternative app.

3. Update software: Ensure that your device is running the latest software version. Go to Settings > Software Update to check for updates.

4. Factory reset: If all else fails, consider performing a factory reset. This will delete all data on your device and return it to its original state. Back up your data before proceeding. To perform a factory reset, go to Settings > General Management > Reset > Factory Data Reset.

Wi-Fi and Bluetooth Connectivity Issues

If you're experiencing issues with Wi-Fi or Bluetooth connectivity, try the following:

1. Toggle Wi-Fi/Bluetooth off and on: Swipe down from the top of the screen to access the Quick Settings panel, and then tap the Wi-Fi or Bluetooth icon to toggle it off and on.

2. Forget and reconnect to the network/device: In the Wi-Fi or Bluetooth settings, select the problematic network or device, and then choose "Forget" or "Unpair." Afterward, reconnect to the network or device.

3. Update software: Ensure that your device is running the latest software version by going to Settings > Software Update.

4. Reset network settings: This will restore your network settings to their default state. To reset network settings, go to Settings > General Management > Reset > Reset Network Settings.

Poor Battery Life

If your Galaxy S23's battery drains quickly, consider the following tips:

1. Lower screen brightness: Swipe down from the top of the screen to access the Quick Settings panel, and then adjust the brightness slider to a lower level.

2. Enable power-saving mode: Go to Settings > Battery and Device Care > Battery > Power Saving Mode, and choose a power-saving mode that suits your needs.

3. Disable unused features: Turn off features like GPS, Bluetooth, Wi-Fi, and NFC when not in use.

4. Monitor battery usage: Check which apps are using the most battery by going to Settings > Battery and Device Care > Battery > Battery Usage.

Camera Issues

If you're experiencing issues with the Galaxy S23's camera, try the following:

1. Clean the camera lens: Use a microfiber cloth to gently clean the camera lens.

2. Restart the device: Press and hold the Power button, then tap "Restart" to reboot the device. This can resolve minor software issues affecting the camera.

3. Check for updates: Make sure your device is running the latest software version by going to Settings > Software Update.

4. Clear the camera app cache and data: Go to Settings > Apps > Camera > Storage, and then tap "Clear Cache" and "Clear Data." This will delete any temporary files and settings related to the camera app but won't affect your photos or videos.

5. Factory reset: If all else fails, consider performing a factory reset. This will delete all data on your device and return it to its original state. Be sure to back up your data before proceeding. To perform a factory reset, go to Settings > General Management > Reset > Factory Data Reset.

Staying Safe and Secure Online

In today's digital age, online safety and security are of utmost importance. In this section, we will discuss various ways to protect your personal information and maintain your privacy while using your Samsung Galaxy S23.

Use Strong Passwords and Biometrics

One of the most fundamental ways to secure your device is by using strong passwords, PINs, or biometrics like fingerprint scanning or facial recognition. To set up or change your device's lock screen security, go to Settings > Lock Screen > Screen Lock Type.

Keep Your Device Updated

Regularly updating your device's software ensures that it has the latest security patches and improvements. To check for updates, go to Settings > Software Update.

Enable Two-Factor Authentication (2FA)

Two-factor authentication adds an extra layer of security to your online accounts by requiring a secondary verification method, such as a text message or authentication app. Enable 2FA for your accounts whenever possible.

Be Cautious with Public Wi-Fi Networks

Public Wi-Fi networks can be convenient, but they can also expose your device to potential security risks. Avoid accessing sensitive information or conducting financial transactions on public networks. If you must use public Wi-Fi, consider using a virtual private network (VPN) to encrypt your internet connection.

Install Reputable Apps

Only install apps from trusted sources, such as the Google Play Store, and research app permissions and reviews before downloading. Be cautious when granting apps access to your personal information and device features.

Secure Your Online Accounts

Use strong, unique passwords for each of your online accounts and change them regularly. Additionally, be cautious with the information you share on social media, and review your privacy settings on a regular basis.

Protect Your Device from Malware

Avoid clicking on suspicious links or downloading attachments from unknown sources. Install a reputable antivirus app on your Galaxy S23 to protect it from malware.

Enable Remote Wipe and Find My Mobile

In case your device is lost or stolen, enabling remote wipe and Find My Mobile can help you locate and protect your personal information. To enable these features, go to Settings > Biometrics and Security > Find My Mobile.

By following the advice in this chapter, you can troubleshoot common issues with your Samsung Galaxy S23 and maintain your online safety and security. Being proactive about your device's maintenance and security will help ensure a smooth, enjoyable experience with your Galaxy S23.

Chapter 4: Communication and Connectivity

In this chapter, we will explore various communication and connectivity features available on the Samsung Galaxy S23. We will discuss how to make and receive calls and texts, use video and voice chat apps, access email and browse the internet, and participate in social media and online communities. By the end of this chapter, you will be well-versed in the different ways you can stay connected with your Samsung Galaxy S23.

Making and Receiving Calls and Texts

The Galaxy S23 is designed to make communication effortless, whether you're making a call, sending a text, or engaging in a group chat. In this section, we'll discuss how to make and receive calls and texts on your device.

Making a Call

To make a call, follow these steps:

1. Open the Phone app from your home screen or app drawer.
2. Enter the phone number using the on-screen keypad or select a contact from your contacts list.
3. Press the green phone icon to initiate the call.

4. To end the call, press the red phone icon.

Receiving a Call

When receiving a call, you have several options:

1. Answer the call by swiping the green phone icon to the right.
2. Decline the call by swiping the red phone icon to the left.
3. Send a quick message to the caller by swiping the message icon upward and selecting a pre-written message or writing your own.

Text Messaging

To send a text message, follow these steps:

1. Open the Messages app from your home screen or app drawer.
2. Tap the compose icon (usually a "+" or a pencil icon) in the bottom right corner.
3. Enter the recipient's phone number or select a contact from your contacts list.
4. Type your message in the text field and tap the send icon.

Using Video and Voice Chat Apps

The Samsung Galaxy S23 supports a variety of video and voice chat apps that enable you to communicate with friends and family, no matter where they are. Some popular apps include WhatsApp, Facebook Messenger, Google Duo, Skype, and Zoom. To use these apps, you'll need to download them from the Google Play Store and sign up for an account if you haven't already.

WhatsApp

WhatsApp is a popular messaging app that offers text, voice, and video chat features. To use WhatsApp, follow these steps:

1. Download and install WhatsApp from the Google Play Store.
2. Open the app and follow the on-screen instructions to create an account.
3. To start a voice or video call, open a chat with the desired contact and tap the phone or video camera icon in the top right corner.

Facebook Messenger

Facebook Messenger is another widely-used messaging app that provides text, voice, and video chat capabilities. To use Facebook Messenger, follow these steps:

1. Download and install Facebook Messenger from the Google Play Store.

2. Open the app and sign in with your Facebook account.

3. To start a voice or video call, select a contact and tap the phone or video camera icon in the top right corner.

Google Duo

Google Duo is a simple and reliable video-calling app available for Android devices. To use Google Duo, follow these steps:

1. Download and install Google Duo from the Google Play Store.

2. Open the app and follow the on-screen instructions to create an account.

3. To start a video call, select a contact and tap the video camera icon.

Skype

Skype is a popular app for voice and video calls, as well as text messaging. To use Skype, follow these steps:

1. Download and install Skype from the Google Play Store.

2. Open the app and sign in or create a new account.

3. To start a voice or video call, select a contact and tap the phone or video camera icon in the top right corner.

Zoom

Zoom is a widely-used video conferencing app that allows you to host or join meetings with multiple participants. To use Zoom, follow these steps:

1. Download and install Zoom from the Google Play Store.

2. Open the app and sign in or create a new account.

3. To start or join a meeting, tap the "New Meeting" or "Join" button and follow the on-screen instructions.

Email and Internet Browsing

The Samsung Galaxy S23 offers convenient access to email and internet browsing. In this section, we'll discuss how to set up your email account and browse the web using your device.

Setting Up Email

To set up your email account on your Galaxy S23, follow these steps:

1. Open the Email app from your home screen or app drawer.
2. If you haven't set up an email account yet, you'll be prompted to add one. Enter your email address and password, and follow the on-screen instructions to complete the setup process.
3. If you need to add another email account, tap the menu icon (usually three lines or dots) in the top left corner, then tap "Add Account" and follow the same steps.

Internet Browsing

To browse the internet on your Galaxy S23, use the pre-installed Samsung Internet browser or download a third-party browser like Google Chrome or Mozilla Firefox from the Google Play Store.

1. Open the browser of your choice from your home screen or app drawer.
2. Enter a URL in the address bar or use the search bar to search for a specific topic.
3. To open a new tab, tap the tab icon (usually represented by a square with a number inside) and then tap the "+" icon.
4. To bookmark a page, tap the menu icon (usually three lines or dots) and select "Add Bookmark" or "Add to Favorites."

Social Media and Online Communities

The Samsung Galaxy S23 provides easy access to various social media platforms and online communities, allowing you to stay connected and engaged with friends, family, and interests. In this section, we'll discuss how to use some popular social media apps and participate in online communities.

Facebook

Facebook is a popular social networking platform that allows you to connect with friends and family, share content, and join groups. To use Facebook, follow these steps:

1. Download and install the Facebook app from the Google Play Store.
2. Open the app and sign in with your Facebook account or create a new one.
3. To post a status update, tap the "What's on your mind?" field at the top of your News Feed and type your message. You can also add photos, videos, or a location to your post.

Instagram

Instagram is a photo and video-sharing app that allows you to connect with friends, celebrities, and interests. To use Instagram, follow these steps:

1. Download and install the Instagram app from the Google Play Store.
2. Open the app and sign in or create a new account.
3. To post a photo or video, tap the "+" icon at the bottom of the screen, select your content, and follow the on-screen instructions to add a caption, location, or tags.

Twitter

Twitter is a microblogging platform that allows you to share short messages, images, and videos and follow others to stay updated on their content. To use Twitter, follow these steps:

1. Download and install the Twitter app from the Google Play Store.
2. Open the app and sign in or create a new account.
3. To post a tweet, tap the compose icon (usually a quill or a "+" symbol) and type your message, keeping in mind the character limit. You can also add photos, videos, or a location to your tweet.

Reddit

Reddit is an online community where users can share content, engage in discussions, and join interest-based groups called "subreddits." To use Reddit, follow these steps:

1. Download and install the Reddit app from the Google Play Store.
2. Open the app and sign in or create a new account.
3. To post a new link or text post, tap the "+" icon at the bottom of the screen and select "Post" or "Link." Choose a subreddit, add a title, and include a URL or text content as needed.
4. To comment on a post, tap the post to open it, and then tap the "Add a comment" field. Type your comment and tap the send icon.

By exploring the various communication and connectivity features of your Samsung Galaxy S23, you can stay connected with friends, family, and interests, no matter where you are. The device's powerful hardware and extensive app support make it a versatile and reliable tool for communication, allowing you to effortlessly make and receive calls, send messages, and engage with online communities.

Chapter 5: Staying Connected

The Samsung Galaxy S23 offers various Samsung-exclusive apps and features to help you stay connected with family and friends, manage your contacts and calendars, and navigate with ease. In this chapter, we will delve into these aspects in detail using Samsung's proprietary apps.

Staying Connected with Family and Friends

Your Samsung Galaxy S23 provides a multitude of ways to stay connected with your loved ones, no matter where they are. In addition to the communication and social media apps discussed in Chapter 4, there are various other Samsung-exclusive apps and features you can use to stay connected:

Samsung Gallery

Samsung Gallery is a photo management app that allows you to view, organize, and share your photos and videos. To use Samsung Gallery, follow these steps:

1. Open the Samsung Gallery app from your home screen or app drawer.
2. Browse your photos and videos by scrolling through the gallery or using the "Albums" view to see your media organized by folder.
3. To share photos with family and friends, select the desired photos, tap the share icon, and choose the recipients or the app through which you want to share.

Samsung Family Hub

Samsung Family Hub is a family communication app that enables you to share calendars, photos, notes, and shopping lists with your family members. To use Samsung Family Hub, follow these steps:

1. Download and install the Samsung Family Hub app from the Galaxy Store.
2. Open the app and create a Samsung account or sign in.
3. Invite your family members to join the app by sending them an invitation code or link.
4. Once your family members have accepted the invitation, you can share and view information within the app.

Managing Contacts and Calendars

Your Samsung Galaxy S23 offers intuitive Samsung tools for managing your contacts and calendars, ensuring you always stay organized and up-to-date.

Managing Contacts

To manage your contacts on your Galaxy S23 using Samsung Contacts, follow these steps:

1. Open the Samsung Contacts app from your home screen or app drawer.
2. To add a new contact, tap the "+" icon and fill in the required information, such as name, phone number, and email address.
3. To edit or delete a contact, tap the contact's name to open their details, then tap the menu icon (usually three dots) in the top right corner and select "Edit" or "Delete."

Managing Calendars

To manage your calendars on your Galaxy S23 using Samsung Calendar, follow these steps:

1. Open the Samsung Calendar app from your home screen or app drawer.
2. To add a new event, tap the "+" icon and fill in the required information, such as the event title, date, time, and location.
3. To edit or delete an event, tap the event to open its details, then tap the menu icon (usually three dots) in the top right corner and select "Edit" or "Delete."

Using GPS and Maps for Navigation

The Samsung Galaxy S23 features built-in GPS and mapping capabilities, allowing you to navigate with ease. In this section, we'll discuss how to use Samsung's navigation app, Here WeGo.

Getting Started with Here WeGo

To use Here WeGo on your Galaxy S23, follow these steps:

1. Ensure that the Here WeGo app is installed on your device. If not, download it from the Galaxy Store.
2. Open the app and allow it to access your device's location.
3. To search for a specific location, use the search bar at the top of the screen and enter the address or name of the place.
4. To get directions, tap the "Directions" button, enter your starting point and destination, and select your preferred mode of transportation (car, public transit, walking, or cycling).

Navigating with Here WeGo

Once you have your route set up, you can use Here WeGo to navigate to your destination. Follow these steps to begin navigating:

1. Tap the "Start" button at the bottom of the screen to begin turn-by-turn navigation.
2. As you drive or walk, Here WeGo will provide voice-guided instructions to help you reach your destination.
3. To view alternate routes, tap the "Routes" button and select a different option.

Real-Time Traffic Information

Here WeGo provides real-time traffic information to help you avoid congestion and choose the most efficient route. To access traffic information, follow these steps:

1. While viewing a map, tap the "Layers" button (usually represented by a stack of squares or circles) in the top right corner of the screen.
2. Select "Traffic" to display traffic conditions on the map. Roads with heavy traffic will be indicated in red, while roads with lighter traffic will be indicated in yellow or green.

Here WeGo Offline

If you need to navigate without an internet connection, you can download maps for offline use. To download an offline map, follow these steps:

1. Open the Here WeGo app and tap the menu icon (usually three lines) in the top left corner.
2. Select "Download maps" and choose the region or country you want to download.
3. Tap "Download" to begin the process.

Location Sharing

Here WeGo allows you to share your real-time location with friends and family. To share your location, follow these steps:

1. Open the Here WeGo app and tap the menu icon (usually three lines) in the top left corner.
2. Select "Share location" and choose the recipients or the app through which you want to share your location.

By utilizing your Samsung Galaxy S23's communication, organization, and navigation features using Samsung's proprietary apps, you can stay connected with family and friends, manage your contacts and calendars, and find your way with ease. The device's intuitive interface and powerful capabilities make it an indispensable tool for maintaining connections and staying organized in today's fast-paced world.

Chapter 6: Advanced Features and Customization

The Samsung Galaxy S23 is packed with advanced features and customization options that allow you to tailor the device to your specific needs and preferences. In this chapter, we will explore these features in detail, focusing on Samsung's proprietary apps and widgets for a seamless experience. Be sure to refer to the Samsung Galaxy S23 User Manual for additional information.

Customizing the Device with Apps and Widgets

Your Samsung Galaxy S23 offers a wide range of apps and widgets to enhance your experience and personalize your device. Here, we will discuss how to add, remove, and customize these elements on your phone.

Adding Apps and Widgets to the Home Screen

To add an app or widget to your home screen, follow these steps:

1. Tap and hold an empty space on the home screen.

2. Select "Widgets" or "Apps" from the menu that appears.

3. Browse the available options by swiping left or right.

4. Tap and hold the app or widget you want to add, then drag it to the desired location on your home screen.

Removing Apps and Widgets from the Home Screen

To remove an app or widget from your home screen, follow these steps:

1. Tap and hold the app or widget you want to remove.

2. Drag the app or widget to the "Remove" or "Trash" icon that appears at the top of the screen.

Customizing App Icons and Folders

The Samsung Galaxy S23 allows you to customize app icons and create folders for better organization. Follow these steps to customize your app icons and folders:

1. Tap and hold an app icon on the home screen.

2. Select "Edit" from the menu that appears.

3. Change the app icon by selecting a new image or choosing from the available options.

4. To create a folder, drag the app icon onto another app icon, then enter a name for the new folder.

Managing and Organizing Files and Media

The Samsung Galaxy S23 makes it easy to manage and organize your files and media, ensuring that you always have quick access to your important documents, photos, and videos. In this section, we will discuss how to use Samsung's proprietary file management app, Samsung My Files.

Navigating Samsung My Files

To navigate Samsung My Files, follow these steps:

1. Open the Samsung My Files app from your home screen or app drawer.

2. Browse your files by selecting one of the categories at the top of the screen (e.g., Images, Videos, Audio, Documents, or Downloads).

3. To search for a specific file, use the search bar at the top of the screen and enter the file name or keyword.

Moving, Copying, and Deleting Files

To move, copy, or delete files using Samsung My Files, follow these steps:

1. Tap and hold the file or files you want to move, copy, or delete.
2. Select the desired action (Move, Copy, or Delete) from the menu that appears at the bottom of the screen.
3. If moving or copying files, navigate to the destination folder and tap "Move here" or "Copy here."

Creating and Managing Folders

To create and manage folders using Samsung My Files, follow these steps:

1. While browsing your files, tap the menu icon (usually three dots) in the top right corner of the screen.
2. Select "Create folder" and enter a name for the new folder.
3. To move files into the new folder, tap and hold the desired files, then select "Move" or "Copy" from the menu and navigate to the new folder.

Managing Cloud Storage

Samsung My Files allows you to connect to various cloud storage services, such as Samsung Cloud, Google Drive, or Microsoft OneDrive. To manage your cloud storage, follow these steps:

1. While using the Samsung My Files app, tap the menu icon (usually three lines) in the top left corner of the screen.
2. Select "Cloud storage" and choose the desired cloud storage service.
3. Sign in to your cloud storage account if prompted.
4. You can now access and manage your cloud files using Samsung My Files, just like you would with files stored locally on your device.

Sharing Files and Media

To share files and media using Samsung My Files, follow these steps:

1. Tap and hold the file or files you want to share.
2. Select the "Share" option from the menu that appears at the bottom of the screen.

3. Choose the recipients or the app through which you want to share the files.

By taking advantage of the advanced features and customization options on your Samsung Galaxy S23, you can create a personalized and efficient experience tailored to your specific needs and preferences. Utilizing Samsung's proprietary apps and widgets, you can easily manage your files and media, customize your home screen, and make the most of your device's powerful capabilities.

Chapter 7: Accessibility and Convenience

The Samsung Galaxy S23 is designed with a wide range of accessibility features and convenient tools that cater to users of all ages, including seniors. In this chapter, we will explore the various accessibility features, mobile payment methods, and health and wellness tools available on the Samsung Galaxy S23.

Accessibility Features for Seniors

Samsung has developed a range of accessibility features to make the Galaxy S23 more user-friendly for seniors and individuals with disabilities. Some of the key accessibility features include:

- Easy Mode: Easy Mode simplifies the user interface, making it easier to navigate and interact with the device. To enable Easy Mode, go to Settings > Display > Easy Mode and toggle the switch on.

- Font Size and Style: Adjust the font size and style to make the text easier to read. To do this, go to Settings > Display > Font size and style, and adjust the settings to your preference.

- Magnification: The Magnification feature allows you to zoom in on certain areas of the screen for better visibility. To enable Magnification, go to Settings > Accessibility > Visibility enhancements > Magnification, and toggle the switch on.

- High-Contrast Themes and Fonts: High-contrast themes and fonts make it easier to see text and icons on the screen. To enable these features, go to Settings > Accessibility > Visibility enhancements, and select the desired options.

- Hearing Aid Compatibility: The Samsung Galaxy S23 is compatible with many hearing aids. To enable this feature, go to Settings > Accessibility > Hearing enhancements > Hearing aid compatibility, and toggle the switch on.

Using Samsung Pay and Other Mobile Payment Methods

The Samsung Galaxy S23 supports Samsung Pay and other mobile payment methods, allowing you to make secure, contactless payments with ease. Here's how to set up and use Samsung Pay on your device:

- Open the Samsung Pay app and sign in with your Samsung account.

- Add a credit or debit card by following the on-screen instructions. You may need to verify your card with your bank.

- To make a payment, open the Samsung Pay app, select the desired card, and authenticate using your fingerprint, face recognition, or PIN.

- Hold your device near the payment terminal, and the transaction will be processed.

Note that other mobile payment methods, such as Google Pay, can also be used on the Samsung Galaxy S23. To set up and use these services, download the respective apps from the Google Play Store and follow the on-screen instructions.

Managing Health and Wellness with the Device

The Samsung Galaxy S23 offers various tools to help you manage your health and wellness. Some of these tools include:

- Samsung Health: The Samsung Health app helps you track your daily activities, monitor your heart rate, measure stress levels, and more. To use Samsung Health, open the app, sign in with your Samsung account, and follow the on-screen instructions to set up your profile and goals.

- Sleep Tracking: Samsung Health also includes a sleep tracking feature that monitors your sleep patterns and provides insights to help improve your sleep quality. To use this feature, wear your Samsung Galaxy S23 while sleeping, and the device will automatically track your sleep data.

- Fitness Tracking: The Samsung Galaxy S23 can track various types of workouts, such as running, cycling, or swimming. To track a workout, open the Samsung Health app, select the "Exercise" tile, and choose the desired workout type.

- Nutrition Tracking: Samsung Health allows you to log your daily food intake and monitor your calorie consumption. To use this feature, open the Samsung Health app, select the "Food" tile, and add your meals and snacks.

- By utilizing the accessibility features, mobile payment methods, and health and wellness tools available on the Samsung Galaxy S23, you can enjoy a more convenient and personalized experience tailored to your needs. These features not only make the device more accessible for seniors and individuals with disabilities but also help users of all ages manage their health and wellness more effectively. The seamless integration of these tools into the Galaxy S23 ensures that you can make the most of your device's capabilities and enjoy a more enriching user experience.

- Stress Management: The Samsung Galaxy S23 can help you monitor and manage stress levels by measuring your heart rate variability. To use this feature, open the Samsung Health app, select the "Stress" tile, and follow the on-screen instructions. The app will provide you with stress level readings and offer suggestions to help you manage stress, such as guided breathing exercises or mindfulness techniques.

- Women's Health: Samsung Health also includes features specifically designed to help women track their menstrual cycles and predict ovulation. To use this feature, open the Samsung Health app, select the "Women's Health" tile, and input the necessary information. The app will then provide you with insights and predictions based on your data.

- Health Reminders: Samsung Health allows you to set reminders for various health-related activities, such as taking medication, drinking water, or engaging in physical activity. To set a reminder, open the Samsung Health app, select the "Reminders" tile, and follow the on-screen instructions to create a custom reminder.

- Health Insights and Recommendations: Samsung Health analyzes your data and provides personalized insights and recommendations to help you reach your health goals. These insights can include suggested workouts, nutrition tips, and sleep improvement strategies.

By taking advantage of the various accessibility and convenience features available on the Samsung Galaxy S23, users of all ages and abilities can enjoy a more inclusive and user-friendly experience. The device's powerful tools not only help you stay connected and manage your health but also make everyday tasks simpler and more efficient. Whether you're a senior or simply looking to make the most of your Galaxy S23, these features are designed to enhance your experience and make your life easier.

Chapter 8: Entertainment and Leisure

The Samsung Galaxy S23 is not just a powerful communication and productivity tool; it also offers a wide range of entertainment and leisure options for users to enjoy. In this chapter, we will explore the various ways you can use your Galaxy S23 for entertainment, including streaming movies and music, playing games, and discovering new hobbies.

Using the Device for Entertainment and Leisure

Streaming Movies and TV Shows

The Samsung Galaxy S23 features a stunning display and powerful processor, making it an excellent device for streaming movies and TV shows. There are several apps you can use to access a vast library of content, such as Netflix, Amazon Prime Video, Hulu, and Disney+. To get started, simply download your preferred streaming app from the Google Play Store and sign in with your account. Then, browse through the available content, choose what you'd like to watch, and enjoy your favorite movies and shows on your Galaxy S23.

Listening to Music and Podcasts

The Galaxy S23 is also a great device for listening to music and podcasts. You can use streaming services like Spotify, Apple Music, YouTube Music, and Amazon Music to access millions of songs, albums, and playlists. Additionally, you can download podcast apps such as Google Podcasts, Spotify, or Pocket Casts to discover and listen to your favorite podcasts. To get started, download your preferred music or podcast app, sign in with your account, and start browsing and listening to your favorite content.

Reading eBooks and Digital Magazines

The Samsung Galaxy S23's large, high-resolution display makes it a suitable device for reading eBooks and digital magazines. You can use apps like Kindle, Google Play Books, or Apple Books to download and read a wide range of eBooks or use apps like Zinio or Readly to access digital magazines. To get started, download your preferred reading app, sign in with your account, and start browsing and reading your favorite books and magazines.

Exploring Virtual Reality (VR) and Augmented Reality (AR)

The Samsung Galaxy S23 supports both Virtual Reality (VR) and Augmented Reality (AR) experiences. VR allows you to immerse yourself in a completely digital world, while AR overlays digital content onto the real world. To experience VR on your Galaxy S23, you can use a compatible VR headset such as the Samsung Gear VR or Google Cardboard. Some popular VR apps and games include YouTube VR, Google Earth VR, and Beat Saber. To enjoy AR experiences on your device, download AR-compatible apps such as Google Lens, Pokémon GO, or IKEA Place from the Google Play Store.

Learning New Skills and Hobbies

The Samsung Galaxy S23 can also be a valuable resource for learning new skills and discovering new hobbies. There are numerous apps available that can help you learn a new language, pick up a musical instrument, practice meditation, or even try your hand at painting or drawing. Some popular learning apps include Duolingo (language learning), Yousician (music lessons), Headspace (meditation), and Procreate (digital art). Download the app that suits your interests, and start exploring new skills and hobbies on your Galaxy S23.

Staying Informed with News Apps

Staying informed about current events and news is essential, and the Samsung Galaxy S23 makes it easy to access the latest information. There are various news apps available for download on the Google Play Store, including CNN, BBC News, The New York Times, and Flipboard. These apps offer personalized news feeds, notifications for breaking news, and the ability to save articles for offline reading. To start using a news app, download your preferred app, sign in with your account (if required), and customize your news preferences to stay up-to-date with the latest happenings around the world.

Socializing through Online Communities

The Galaxy S23 can also help you stay connected with like-minded individuals through online communities and forums. Apps like Reddit, Quora, and Amino allow you to join discussions, share your thoughts, and connect with others who share your interests. Whether you're looking for advice, wanting to share your expertise, or simply seeking a supportive community, these apps offer various options to engage with others online. Download your preferred app, create an account, and start exploring the different communities and forums available.

Relaxing with Meditation and Mindfulness Apps

In today's fast-paced world, it's important to find moments of relaxation and mindfulness. The Samsung Galaxy S23 offers various apps designed to help you practice meditation, reduce stress, and improve your overall mental well-being. Apps like Calm, Headspace, and Insight Timer offer guided meditations, sleep stories, and mindfulness exercises to help you find balance and peace in your daily life. Download your preferred app, sign in with your account, and start exploring the different meditation and mindfulness exercises available.

In conclusion, the Samsung Galaxy S23 offers a diverse range of entertainment and leisure options that cater to a variety of interests and hobbies. By exploring the various apps and features available on your device, you can discover new ways to enjoy your free time, learn new skills, and stay connected with friends, family, and online communities. With the Samsung Galaxy S23, the possibilities for entertainment and leisure are virtually endless.

Chapter 9: Updates and Upgrades

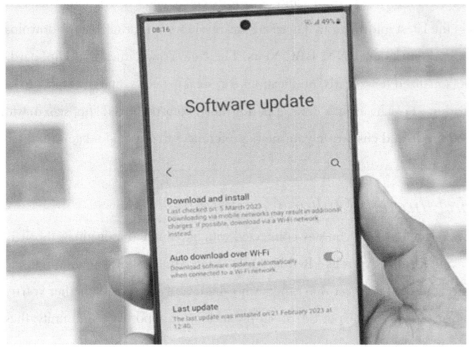

Keeping your Samsung Galaxy S23 up-to-date with the latest software updates and upgrades is crucial for ensuring the best performance, security, and overall user experience. In this chapter, we will discuss the importance of updates, how to check for updates, and what to expect from future upgrades.

Staying Up-to-Date with the Latest Updates and Upgrades

The Importance of Updates and Upgrades

Updates and upgrades serve a variety of purposes, including:

- Improving the overall performance and stability of your device
- Fixing bugs and addressing security vulnerabilities
- Introducing new features and enhancements
- Optimizing battery life and performance

- Ensuring compatibility with the latest apps and services
- By staying up-to-date with the latest updates and upgrades, you can ensure that your Samsung Galaxy S23 remains secure, efficient, and enjoyable to use.

Checking for Updates on Your Samsung Galaxy S23

To check for updates on your Galaxy S23, follow these steps:

1. Open the "Settings" app on your device.
2. Scroll down and tap on "Software update."
3. Tap on "Download and install" to check for available updates.
4. If an update is available, your device will automatically download and install it. Depending on the size of the update and your internet connection, this process may take some time. Make sure your device is connected to a Wi-Fi network and has sufficient battery life before proceeding with an update.

Understanding the Update Process

When an update is available for your Galaxy S23, you will receive a notification informing you of the update. You can choose to install the update immediately or schedule it for a later time. It's essential to ensure that your device has enough battery life or is connected to a charger before starting the update process, as interruptions can cause issues.

During the update process, your device will restart, and you will see an update progress screen. Do not turn off your device or interrupt the update process, as this can cause issues and potentially damage your device.

What to Expect from Future Upgrades

As a Samsung Galaxy S23 user, you can expect regular updates and upgrades from Samsung. These updates may include the following:

- Security patches: Samsung releases monthly security patches to address any potential vulnerabilities and ensure that your device remains secure.
- Feature updates: Occasionally, Samsung may introduce new features or enhancements to existing features through software updates. These updates can improve the overall user experience and offer additional functionality.

- Android version upgrades: Samsung typically supports its flagship devices for at least two major Android version upgrades. This means that your Galaxy S23 will likely receive upgrades to future versions of Android, ensuring compatibility with the latest apps and services.

Participating in the Samsung Members App

The Samsung Members app is an excellent resource for staying informed about updates and getting support for your Galaxy S23. The app allows you to:

- Receive news and announcements about updates and new features
- Access support resources and troubleshooting guides
- Participate in community forums and discussions with other Samsung users
- Provide feedback on your device and report any issues
- By participating in the Samsung Members app, you can stay informed about the latest updates and upgrades, get support for your device, and connect with other Samsung users.

In conclusion, staying up-to-date with the latest updates and upgrades is essential for ensuring the best possible experience with your Samsung Galaxy S23. By regularly checking for updates and understanding the update process, you can keep your device secure, efficient, and enjoyable to use. With ongoing support from Samsung, you can expect regular updates and upgrades that will continue to enhance your Galaxy S23 experience.

Chapter 10: Home Automation and Smart Devices

In this chapter, we will explore how to connect your Samsung Galaxy S23 to various smart home devices and use your smartphone to control your home environment. With advancements in technology, the Galaxy S23 can now act as a central hub for managing and controlling various smart devices in your home, making your life more comfortable and convenient.

Connecting Your Samsung Galaxy S23 to Smart Home Devices

The Samsung Galaxy S23 is a powerful device that can help you manage and control various aspects of your smart home. By connecting your smartphone to compatible smart devices, you can create a centralized hub for controlling your home environment, making it more comfortable and convenient. In this section, we will provide a detailed guide on how to connect your Galaxy S23 to different smart home devices.

Compatibility and Required Apps

Before attempting to connect your Galaxy S23 to a smart home device, it's essential to ensure that the device is compatible with your smartphone. Most smart home devices use Wi-Fi or Bluetooth to connect with smartphones, and many have dedicated apps available on the Google Play Store. To find out if your smart device is compatible with the Galaxy S23, check the device's documentation or visit the manufacturer's website.

Once you have confirmed compatibility, download and install the dedicated app for your smart home device from the Google Play Store. This app will serve as the primary interface for controlling and managing your smart device using your Galaxy S23.

Connecting to Wi-Fi and Pairing Mode

To connect your Galaxy S23 to a smart home device, you first need to ensure that the device is connected to your home Wi-Fi network (if necessary) and is in pairing mode. Connecting your smart device to Wi-Fi is typically done during the initial setup process using the device's dedicated app. Consult your smart device's user manual for specific instructions on connecting it to Wi-Fi. Next, put your smart device in pairing mode. This process varies between devices, so refer to the user manual or manufacturer's website for detailed instructions. In general, pairing mode is activated by pressing a button or a combination of buttons on the device or through the dedicated app.

Connecting Your Galaxy S23 to the Smart Device

Now that your smart device is connected to Wi-Fi and in pairing mode follow these steps to connect your Galaxy S23 to the device:

1. Open the dedicated app for your smart home device on your Galaxy S23.
2. Follow the on-screen instructions to create an account (if required) and sign in.
3. The app should automatically detect nearby devices that are in pairing mode. If not, there may be an option to manually search for available devices or enter a pairing code.
4. Select your smart device from the list and confirm the connection when prompted.

Once your Galaxy S23 is connected to the smart home device, you will be able to control and manage the device through its dedicated app.

Setting up Multiple Devices and Smart Home Hubs

If you have multiple smart home devices, you may need to repeat the above process for each device. However, some devices may require a smart home hub to connect and manage multiple devices from a single interface. Smart home hubs, such as Samsung SmartThings or Amazon Echo, can simplify the process of connecting and controlling multiple smart devices in your home.

To connect your Galaxy S23 to a smart home hub, follow the hub's specific setup instructions, which typically involve downloading a dedicated app, creating an account, and connecting the hub to your Wi-Fi network. Once your hub is set up, you can use it to connect and control multiple smart devices in your home through a single interface.

Controlling Your Home Environment with Your Smartphone

With your Samsung Galaxy S23 connected to your smart home devices, you can now use your smartphone to control various aspects of your home environment. Some examples of smart home devices and their functions include:

Smart Lighting

Smart lighting systems allow you to control the brightness, color, and schedule of your home's lights using your smartphone. By connecting your Galaxy S23 to a compatible smart lighting system, you can:

1. Turn your lights on and off remotely
2. Adjust the brightness and color of your lights
3. Set schedules for your lights to turn on and off automatically
4. Create custom lighting scenes for different moods or activities

Smart Thermostats

A smart thermostat can help you manage your home's temperature more efficiently and save energy. With a smart thermostat connected to your Galaxy S23, you can:

1. Adjust your home's temperature remotely
2. Set schedules for temperature changes throughout the day
3. Monitor your energy usage and make adjustments to save energy

4. Receive notifications if your home's temperature goes outside of a set range

Smart Security Systems

Smart security systems can provide peace of mind by allowing you to monitor your home remotely and receive alerts if any security issues arise. By connecting your Galaxy S23 to a smart security system, you can:

1. Monitor live video feeds from security cameras
2. Receive notifications if motion or sound is detected
3. Control smart locks and grant or revoke access to your home
4. Manage alarms and other security features remotely

Smart Home Appliances

Many modern home appliances now come with smart features, allowing you to control them using your Galaxy S23. Examples of smart appliances include:

1. Smart refrigerators that can track inventory and create shopping lists
2. Smart ovens that can be controlled remotely and offer cooking guidance
3. Smart washing machines that can be started remotely and provide maintenance alerts
4. Smart vacuum cleaners that can be scheduled and controlled using your smartphone

Using Samsung SmartThings

Samsung offers its own smart home ecosystem called SmartThings, which allows you to control a wide range of smart devices using a single app on your Galaxy S23. To set up and use SmartThings, follow these steps:

- Download and install the SmartThings app from the Google Play Store.
- Open the app and sign in with your Samsung account (or create one if you don't have one).
- Follow the on-screen instructions to set up your SmartThings Hub (if required) and connect your compatible smart devices.
- Once your devices are connected, you can use the SmartThings app to control and monitor them from your Galaxy S23.

The SmartThings app provides a centralized interface for managing and controlling various smart devices in your home. You can create routines, set schedules, and automate actions based on specific conditions. Some examples of automation using SmartThings include:

- Turning on lights when you arrive home
- Adjusting the thermostat based on the time of day or occupancy
- Locking your doors automatically when you leave home
- Sending a notification if a security camera detects motion
- Integrating Your Smart Home with Voice Assistants

To further enhance your smart home experience, you can integrate your Samsung Galaxy S23 with voice assistants like Google Assistant or Bixby. This allows you to control your smart devices using voice commands, making it even more convenient to manage your home environment. To set up voice control for your smart home devices, follow these steps:

- For Google Assistant: Open the Google Home app on your Galaxy S23 and sign in with your Google account. Tap on the "+" icon and select "Set up the device," then choose "Works with Google" and find your smart device's app from the list. Follow the on-screen instructions to link your smart device account with Google Assistant.
- For Bixby: Open the Bixby app on your Galaxy S23 and sign in with your Samsung account. Tap on the menu icon (three lines) and select "Capsules." Search for your smart device's app and tap on it to link your smart device account with Bixby.

Once you have set up voice control, you can use commands like "Hey Google, turn on the living room lights" or "Hi Bixby, set the thermostat to 72 degrees" to control your smart home devices using your Galaxy S23.

In conclusion, the Samsung Galaxy S23 offers a versatile and powerful platform for managing and controlling your smart home devices. By connecting your smartphone to various smart devices, you can create a more comfortable, convenient, and efficient living environment. With the help of Samsung SmartThings and voice assistants, you can further enhance your smart home experience and enjoy the benefits of home automation.

Chapter 11: Tips and Tricks for Efficient Smartphone Use

The Samsung Galaxy S23 is a powerful and feature-rich smartphone designed to make your life more efficient and enjoyable. With a plethora of built-in features, apps, and customization options, you can streamline your day-to-day tasks and get the most out of your device. In this chapter, we will explore helpful shortcuts, gestures, and tips for maximizing productivity with your Samsung Galaxy S23.

Helpful Shortcuts and Gestures

The Galaxy S23 includes numerous shortcuts and gestures that make it easier to access your favorite apps, settings, and features. Here are some of the most useful shortcuts and gestures to help you navigate your smartphone more efficiently:

a. Quick Launch Camera: To quickly launch the camera, press the power button twice. This shortcut allows you to capture important moments without having to unlock your phone or search for the camera app.

b. One-Handed Mode: To enable one-handed mode, swipe down from the bottom edge of the screen and release your finger. This gesture reduces the screen size, making it easier to use your phone with one hand.

c. Edge Panels: Swipe inwards from the edge of the screen to access Edge panels, which provide quick access to your favorite apps, contacts, and features.

d. Swipe to Call or Text: In the Contacts app, swipe right on a contact to call them or swipe left to send a text message.

e. Split Screen: To use two apps simultaneously, open the first app and then swipe up from the bottom of the screen to open the Recents menu. Tap the app icon and select "Open in split-screen view." Then, choose the second app you want to use.

f. Smart Pop-up View: When you receive a notification, tap and drag the notification down to open the app in a small pop-up window, allowing you to multitask without leaving your current app.

Customizing Your Home Screen

Your home screen is the main hub of your Galaxy S23, and customizing it to suit your needs can greatly enhance your smartphone experience. Here are some tips for personalizing your home screen:

a. Organize apps into folders: To create a folder, tap and hold an app icon, then drag it over another app icon and release. You can then add more apps to the folder and rename it by tapping the folder and selecting the folder name.

b. Add widgets: Widgets provide quick access to app information and function directly from your home screen. To add a widget, tap and hold an empty area of the home screen, then select "Widgets." Browse the available widgets and tap the one you want to add. Drag it to the desired location on your home screen and release.

c. Change your wallpaper: To set a new wallpaper, tap and hold an empty area of the home screen, then select "Wallpapers." You can choose from preloaded wallpapers, your own photos, or download new wallpapers from the Galaxy Store.

d. Customize the app grid: To change the number of apps displayed on your home screen, tap and hold an empty area of the home screen, then select "Home screen settings." Choose "Home screen grid" or "Apps screen grid" and select the grid size you prefer.

Maximizing Productivity with Your Samsung Galaxy S23

The Galaxy S23 is packed with features designed to help you stay organized, focused, and productive. Here are some tips to help you get the most out of your device:

a. Utilize the Calendar app: The built-in Calendar app allows you to create events, set reminders, and view your schedule at a glance. Sync your calendar with other devices and accounts to keep all your events and appointments in one place.

b. Set up Do Not Disturb mode: To minimize distractions during important tasks or meetings, enable Do Not Disturb mode. Swipe down from the top of the screen to access the Quick Settings panel, then tap the "Do Not Disturb" icon. You can also schedule specific times for Do Not Disturb mode to activate automatically by going to Settings > Sounds and Vibration> Do Not Disturb.

c. Use Bixby Routines: Bixby Routines automate certain actions based on your location, time, or device usage. To set up a routine, go to Settings > Advanced features > Bixby Routines. Tap the "+" button to create a new routine, select the conditions and actions you want, and save your routine. Bixby Routines can help you save time and energy by automating tasks such as enabling Wi-Fi when you're at home or silencing your phone during work hours.

d. Take advantage of Samsung Notes: The Samsung Notes app is a versatile tool for creating and organizing text, images, and audio notes. Use it to jot down ideas, create to-do lists, or record voice memos. You can also sync your notes across devices to access them anywhere.

e. Utilize the Reminders app: To create and manage reminders, open the Reminders app and tap the "+" button to add a new reminder. You can set a due date and location or attach images to your reminder. You can also add reminders directly from other apps, such as the Calendar or Samsung Notes app.

f. Use the Edge Lighting feature: Edge Lighting provides visual notifications for incoming messages and calls, even when your screen is off. To enable Edge Lighting, go to Settings > Display > Edge screen > Edge Lighting. Customize the lighting effect, color, and duration to suit your preferences.

Enhance Your Galaxy S23 with Accessories and Third-Party Apps

To further improve your Galaxy S23 experience, consider investing in accessories or downloading third-party apps:

a. Wireless charging: The Galaxy S23 supports wireless charging, allowing you to charge your phone without dealing with cables. Purchase a compatible wireless charging pad to take advantage of this feature.

b. Samsung DeX: Samsung DeX lets you connect your Galaxy S23 to an external display, keyboard, and mouse for a desktop-like experience. Purchase a compatible DeX cable or wireless DeX adapter to use this feature.

c. Download productivity apps: There are countless productivity apps available on the Google Play Store that can help you stay organized, focused, and efficient. Some popular options include Todoist, Evernote, and Trello.

In conclusion, the Samsung Galaxy S23 offers numerous features, shortcuts, and gestures that can help you maximize productivity and efficiency. By customizing your home screen, taking advantage of built-in apps and settings, and exploring third-party solutions, you can get the most out of your smartphone and streamline your daily tasks.

FAQ

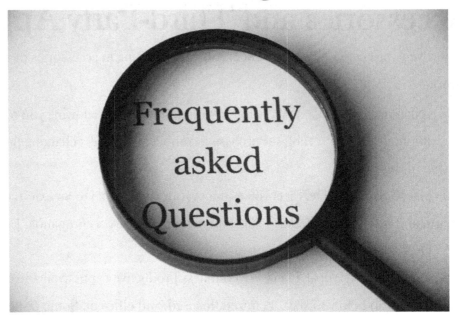

Q: How can I increase the text size on my Samsung Galaxy S23 to make it easier to read?

A: To increase the text size, go to Settings > Display > Font size and style, and adjust the font size slider to your preferred size.

Q: Can I use voice commands on my Galaxy S23 to make calls and send messages without touching the screen?

A: Yes, you can use Google Assistant or Bixby to perform tasks like making calls and sending messages using voice commands.

Q: What are some essential accessibility features available on the Samsung Galaxy S23 for seniors?

A: Some important accessibility features include magnification, high contrast theme, font adjustments, and hearing aid compatibility.

Q: How do I set up a mobile payment method like Samsung Pay on my Galaxy S23?

A: To set up Samsung Pay, open the Samsung Pay app, sign in with your Samsung account, and follow the on-screen instructions to add your credit or debit card.

Q: Is it possible to use the Samsung Galaxy S23 to track my health and wellness activities?

A: Yes, you can use the Samsung Health app to monitor your daily activities, heart rate, sleep patterns, and more.

Q: How do I connect my Samsung Galaxy S23 to my smart home devices?

A: You can connect your smartphone to compatible smart home devices using apps like SmartThings or Google Home, depending on the devices you have.

Q: How do I enable Android Auto on my Samsung Galaxy S23 to use it with my car's infotainment system?

A: To enable Android Auto, download and install the Android Auto app, connect your phone to your car using a USB cable, and follow the on-screen prompts.

Q: How can I manage and organize my files and media on the Samsung Galaxy S23?

A: You can use the built-in My Files app to organize, move, and delete files or use the Gallery app to manage your photos and videos.

Q: What are some tips for taking better photos with the Samsung Galaxy S23's camera?

A: Some tips include using the appropriate camera mode, adjusting exposure and focus, and utilizing features like Night mode and Pro mode for better results.

Q: How do I keep my Samsung Galaxy S23 updated with the latest software and security patches?

A: To check for updates, go to Settings > Software update > Download and install. Your device will search for available updates and prompt you to install them.

Q: How do I customize the look and feel of my Samsung Galaxy S23's home screen?

A: You can customize your home screen by long-pressing on an empty space, then selecting themes, wallpapers, and widgets, or adjusting the grid size to suit your preferences.

Q: How do I enable the one-handed mode on my Samsung Galaxy S23 to make it easier to use with one hand?

A: To enable one-handed mode, go to Settings > Advanced features > One-handed mode and toggle the switch on. You can then activate it by swiping down diagonally from either bottom corner of the screen.

Q: Can I create a shortcut for frequently used settings on my Samsung Galaxy S23?

A: Yes, you can add shortcuts to frequently used settings in the notification panel by swiping down from the top of the screen and tapping the three-dot menu icon, then selecting "Button order" to customize the available shortcuts.

Q: How do I enable Do Not Disturb mode on my Samsung Galaxy S23 to avoid interruptions?

A: To enable Do Not Disturb mode, swipe down from the top of the screen to access the notification panel, and tap the "Do Not Disturb" icon. You can also set a schedule or customize exceptions in the Settings > Sounds and Vibration> Do Not Disturb menu.

Q: How do I transfer my data from my old phone to my new Samsung Galaxy S23?

A: You can use the Samsung Smart Switch app to transfer your data from your old device to your new Galaxy S23. Download the app on both devices, follow the on-screen instructions, and select the data you want to transfer.

Bonus: Android Auto in Your Car

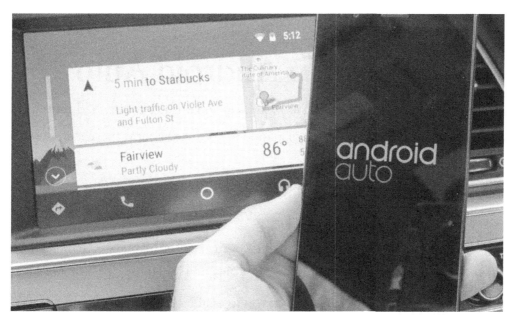

Android Auto is a powerful and convenient way to integrate your Samsung Galaxy S23 with your car's infotainment system, making it easier to access your favorite apps, navigation, and media while driving. In this chapter, we'll explore the features and benefits of Android Auto, how to set it up, and tips for using it safely and effectively.

Overview of Android Auto

Android Auto is a mobile app developed by Google that enables you to connect your smartphone to your car's infotainment system. With Android Auto, you can access your phone's apps, messages, music, and navigation on your car's display, allowing you to stay connected and informed while keeping your hands on the wheel and your eyes on the road.

Key features of Android Auto include:

- Navigation: Access Google Maps or Waze for turn-by-turn directions and real-time traffic updates.
- Music and media: Stream your favorite music, podcasts, and audiobooks from popular apps like Spotify, Google Play Music, and Amazon Music.

- Voice control: Use Google Assistant to control various functions, such as sending text messages, making phone calls, or finding nearby points of interest.

- Notifications: Receive and respond to messages and notifications from supported messaging apps, like WhatsApp and Facebook Messenger, using voice commands or quick replies.

Setting Up Android Auto

To use Android Auto, you'll need a compatible vehicle, a Samsung Galaxy S23 running Android 10 or later, and a USB cable to connect your phone to your car. Follow these steps to set up Android Auto:

1. Download the Android Auto app: Install the Android Auto app on your Galaxy S23 from the Google Play Store.

2. Enable Android Auto in your car: Consult your car's user manual or manufacturer's website to find out if your vehicle supports Android Auto and how to enable it in your infotainment system. Some cars require you to enable Android Auto through the car's settings menu, while others may automatically detect your phone once it's connected.

3. Connect your Galaxy S23 to your car: Using a high-quality USB cable, connect your phone to your car's USB port. Your car's display should recognize your phone and display the Android Auto interface.

4. Grant permissions: The first time you connect your phone, you'll need to grant Android Auto permission to access various features and apps on your device. Follow the on-screen prompts to complete the setup process.

Navigating the Android Auto Interface

Once connected, your car's display will show the Android Auto home screen, which consists of a series of app icons and a Google Assistant microphone button. The interface is designed for easy navigation while driving, with large icons and simplified menus.

Here are the main sections of the Android Auto interface:

- Home screen: The home screen displays an overview of your current activity, such as ongoing navigation or media playback, as well as suggested destinations and recent calls or messages.

- Navigation: Tap the navigation icon to access Google Maps or Waze, depending on your preference. You can search for destinations, view real-time traffic information, and receive turn-by-turn directions.

- Media: Tap the media icon to browse and control your music, podcasts, or audiobooks from supported apps like Spotify, Google Play Music, or Amazon Music.

- Phone: Tap the phone icon to access your recent calls, contacts, and voicemail. You can also use voice commands to initiate phone calls.

- Notifications: When you receive a message or notification, Android Auto will display a pop-up at the top of the screen. Tap the notification to have the message read aloud or to reply using voice commands.

Tips for Using Android Auto Safely and Effectively

While Android Auto is designed to enhance your driving experience, it's crucial to use it responsibly and prioritize safety. Here are some tips for using Android Auto safely and effectively:

- Familiarize yourself with the interface: Before hitting the road, spend some time exploring Android Auto's interface and features while your car is parked. This will help you navigate the system more efficiently and confidently when driving.

- Use voice commands: Google Assistant is a valuable feature of Android Auto, allowing you to control various functions with your voice. To activate Google Assistant, press and hold the microphone button on your car's display or steering wheel (if equipped) and speak your command. You can ask Google Assistant to make phone calls, send messages, play music, or find nearby points of interest.

- Limit app usage: While it's tempting to access all of your favorite apps while driving, it's essential to prioritize safety and minimize distractions. Stick to essential apps like navigation, music, and messaging, and avoid using other apps that may require more attention.

- Customize settings for a better experience: You can adjust Android Auto's settings to better suit your needs and preferences. For example, you can enable or disable message previews, choose your preferred navigation app, or adjust the volume levels for different types of audio.

- Keep your phone and apps updated: To ensure the best possible experience with Android Auto, make sure your Galaxy S23 is running the latest version of Android, and keep your apps up to date. This will ensure compatibility and access to the latest features and improvements.

- Use a high-quality USB cable: A reliable, high-quality USB cable is essential for a stable connection between your phone and your car. Poor-quality cables may cause intermittent disconnections or charging issues.

Troubleshooting Android Auto

If you encounter issues with Android Auto, try the following troubleshooting steps:

1. Check your USB cable: A faulty or low-quality USB cable can cause connection problems. Make sure you're using a high-quality cable and try a different one if issues persist.

2. Restart your phone and car: Sometimes, simply restarting your phone and turning your car off and on again can resolve connectivity issues.

3. Update your software: Ensure your Galaxy S23 is running the latest version of Android and your car's infotainment system has the most recent firmware. Consult your car's user manual or manufacturer's website for information on updating your infotainment system.

4. Clear the Android Auto app's cache: If you're experiencing performance issues or crashes, try clearing the cache for the Android Auto app. Go to Settings > Apps > Android Auto > Storage > Clear cache.

5. Reset Android Auto settings: If all else fails, you can reset Android Auto's settings by going to Settings > Apps > Android Auto > Storage > Clear data. Keep in mind that this will erase your preferences and require you to set up Android Auto again.

In conclusion, Android Auto offers a seamless way to integrate your Samsung Galaxy S23 with your car's infotainment system, providing access to navigation, media, and communication features while prioritizing safety. By setting up Android Auto, familiarizing yourself with its interface and following best practices, you can enhance your driving experience and stay connected on the go.

Conclusion

In conclusion, the Samsung Galaxy S23 for Seniors is a comprehensive guide designed to help seniors and non-tech-savvy users make the most of their brand-new smartphone. This book covers everything from the initial setup and customization of the device to mastering advanced features and ensuring online safety. With detailed instructions, tips, and tricks, you'll gain the confidence to navigate your Galaxy S23 with ease, transforming it into an indispensable tool for staying connected with family and friends, managing your daily activities, and enjoying a wealth of entertainment options.

As technology continues to advance, it becomes increasingly important for seniors to adapt and embrace the benefits that smartphones like the Galaxy S23 have to offer. By making use of the various features and functions outlined in this book, you'll be able to stay informed, connected, and entertained, enhancing your overall quality of life.

We hope that this book has provided you with the skills necessary and knowledge to make the most of your Samsung Galaxy S23. Remember that practice makes perfect, and the more you use your smartphone, the more comfortable and proficient you will become. Don't hesitate to refer back to this guide as needed, and consider sharing your newfound expertise with friends and family who may also benefit from the Galaxy S23's features.

Thank you for choosing the Samsung Galaxy S23 for Seniors as your companion on this exciting journey into the world of modern technology. We wish you many enjoyable and rewarding experiences with your new smartphone.

Index Table